T4-ADP-719

The Question & Answer Book

WONDERS OF WATER

WONDERS OF WATER

By Jane Dickinson
Illustrated by Rex Schneider

Troll Associates

Library of Congress Cataloging in Publication Data

Dickinson, Jane.
　　Wonders of water.

　　(The Question and answer book)
　　Summary: Answers such questions as "Where does water
come from?" and "Why is the ocean salty?" Includes
simple experiments.
　　1. Water—Juvenile literature. [1. Water. 2. Questions and answers] I. Schneider, Rex, ill. II. Title.
III. Series.
GB662.3.D52　1983　　　551.4　　　82-17388
ISBN 0-89375-874-4
ISBN 0-89375-875-2 (pbk.)

Copyright © 1983 by Troll Associates, Mahwah, New Jersey

All rights reserved. No part of this book may be used
or reproduced in any manner whatsoever without written
permission from the publisher.

Printed in the United States of America
10　　9　　8　　7　　6　　5　　4　　3　　2

Where is water?

Water seems to be just about everywhere. There is water in oceans, rivers, and lakes. There is water in clouds and in the air. There is water in an icicle and in a lump of mud. There is water in a snowball and in an orange. And there is water in you. Your body is about two-thirds water!

Water is always changing.

Sometimes water is solid, like an ice cube. Sometimes it is a gas that you cannot see. Most often, it is a liquid, like the water in a river. In its liquid form alone, there is so much water that it covers almost three-fourths of the Earth.

Plants have a great deal of water in them. Some are nearly eighty percent water. You can try a simple experiment to prove that plants have water in them.

Break a carrot or a piece of celery in half, and touch the broken ends. You will see that they are wet. Break the leaf of a plant. The broken edge will be damp—even though the rest of the plant seems dry.

All living things have water in them.

If living things do not get enough water, they will die. So they must take in water in some way. Plants take it in through their roots. Animals drink water. So do people.

Where does water come from?

If we use so much of it every day, why isn't it all gone? Why don't we ever seem to run out of water?

The answer is that most of our water supply never really goes away. We use it over and over again. After you take a bath, the water goes down the drain. Is it lost forever? No. It will be used again some day—somewhere on the Earth. But first, it must take a long trip—in a kind of circle scientists call the *water cycle*.

Along its way in the water cycle, your bath water changes its form several times. It flows from the bathtub through pipes and eventually to the ocean. From the surface of the ocean, it turns into a gas and rises into the air. Then it falls to the Earth as rain or snow. It may seep into the earth and enter an underground well. Or it may flow along the surface of the Earth and enter a reservoir. And someday, it could enter the pipes in your house and be used again.

Let's see what happens in each part of the water cycle. Ninety-seven percent of the Earth's water is in the ocean, so that's a good place to start. Water *evaporates* from the ocean all the time. This means it becomes an invisible gas called *water vapor*. Here's how it happens.

Water is made up of tiny bits of matter called *water molecules.* These molecules are so tiny that a tablespoon of water contains about a trillion of them. Water molecules are always moving—pushing and bumping into one another. Heat makes them move even faster. They bump into each other with greater force than when they are cold.

As the sun warms the surface of the ocean, the water molecules heat up. They begin to move faster. The fast-moving water molecules push and bump against each other hard enough to fly into the air. Once in the air, they become water vapor.

How do clouds form?

Warm air, with water vapor in it, rises up from the ocean. As the air rises, it gets colder. The water vapor molecules in the air get colder, too. They move more slowly, and they pull closer together. When they get very cold—and very close together—they *condense.* This means they change into tiny droplets of water. That's how clouds form.

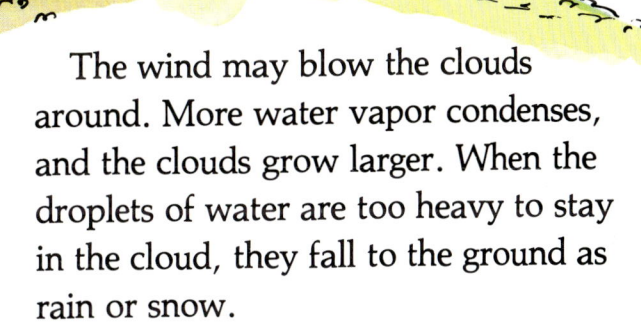

The wind may blow the clouds around. More water vapor condenses, and the clouds grow larger. When the droplets of water are too heavy to stay in the cloud, they fall to the ground as rain or snow.

How do we get the water we use?

Rain or melting snow that seeps into the ground is called *ground water.* It gets trapped between rocks and forms underground pools. If pipes are put down into underground pools, the pools are called wells. Pumping the wells forces the ground water up through the pipes and into people's homes.

When water does not seep into the ground, it may flow into rivers, lakes, and *reservoirs.* A reservoir is a lake where water is collected and stored. It is like a savings bank for water. Cities usually get their water supplies from reservoirs instead of from wells.

Huge pipes called *aqueducts* carry the water from a reservoir to a city. Some aqueducts are so big that a truck could drive through them. Near the city, the water is piped into treatment plants, where it is cleaned and purified. From there, it is pumped into smaller pipes. They are called *water mains.* The water mains have branches, or smaller pipes, that go to every street and building in the city.

What happens when water evaporates from your skin?

Have you ever noticed that you sometimes shiver on a hot day after you come out from swimming? This is because the water on your skin is evaporating. As water evaporates, it takes heat away from your body. This makes you feel cold. *Any surface is cooled when water evaporates from it.*

The next experiment will prove that *water evaporates off the surface of a body of water.* You will need a wide bowl, a drinking glass, and a narrow jar, like an olive jar. Pour the same amount of water into each container. Mark the water level on the outside of each container with a crayon or a piece of tape. Then put the containers aside for a day, but do not cover them.

After one day, look at the water level in each container. You will see that the water in the wide bowl has evaporated more than the other "bodies of water." That's because the water in that bowl has a bigger surface area. There is more space from which the molecules can escape and turn into water vapor. The water in the narrow jar has evaporated the least. That "body of water" has the smallest surface area.

Try these experiments.

Here are some simple experiments you can do to find out about evaporation. First, wet two pieces of cloth of about the same size. Then spread one piece on a warm radiator, or out in the hot sun. Spread the other one on a counter top in your kitchen.

About an hour later, look at the two pieces of cloth. Which one is dry or almost dry? You should find that the one in the warm place—on the radiator or in the hot sunshine—is dry. Do you know why this happened? It happened because *water evaporates faster when it is heated.* Molecules of water move faster—and turn into water vapor more quickly—when they are heated.

When you want to take a bath, you turn on a faucet. Water from a reservoir or from a well is pumped through the pipes and fills your bathtub. Then, after you take your bath, the water goes down the drain. It joins other waste water, called sewage. The sewage flows through bigger pipes called sewers. Most cities treat their sewage and make the waste water clean. Then the water is pumped back into lakes or rivers. Eventually, it reaches the sea. The water cycle has made a full circle. But the water cycle does not stop there—it is repeated over and over again.

Water also evaporates from other places besides the oceans. It evaporates from lakes, reservoirs, ponds, and even from puddles. In fact, wherever water is next to air, evaporation takes place.

What happens when water vapor cools?

When water vapor cools, it condenses back into water. It changes from an invisible gas back to a liquid. Here is an easy experiment you can do to prove this.

Take two empty drinking glasses that are the same size. Fill one with warm water. Fill the other one with several ice cubes and cold water. In a few minutes, what do you see?

The outside of the cold glass has become wet. But nothing has happened to the outside of the warm glass. Where did the wetness on the cold glass come from? It came from water vapor in the air. When water vapor touched the cold glass, the vapor began to cool off. Its molecules moved more slowly, and pulled closer together. Then the water vapor condensed back into water.

Have you ever seen people breathe on their eyeglasses before wiping them clean? Their eyeglasses are colder than their breath. The warm water vapor in their breath condenses on the cold glasses. It makes just enough water to clean them.

Did you ever see your own breath turn into a cloud on a cold day?

The cloud was made of tiny droplets of water. Invisible water vapor in your warm breath condensed into tiny droplets of water when it hit the cold air.

Cold air changes the gas called water vapor to a liquid form. *Very* cold air can do something else. It can change water from a liquid to a solid form. Did you ever fall on ice? If so, you know just how solid ice can be! Ice is really frozen water, or water in its solid form.

When water freezes, a strange thing happens. It takes up more space. Ice takes up more space than water in its liquid form. So water *expands* when it freezes—it grows slightly bigger.

Here is an experiment that will prove this. Fill a cardboard milk container with water. Fill it to the very top, and seal it with tape. Then put the carton in a plastic bag and seal that, too. Put the filled carton into your kitchen freezer. The next day, take it out and see what has happened. You should see that the cardboard container has split open. What caused this?

The very cold air in the freezer turned the water to ice. As the water turned to ice, it expanded. The ice needed more space than the water, so it pushed out the top or the sides of the milk carton.

19

When water freezes, it pushes very hard in all directions. It can even push hard enough to break up a concrete sidewalk. Do you know how? When it rains, water seeps down into the cracks of a sidewalk. Then, if the weather is cold, the water turns to ice. As the water freezes, it expands. It pushes hard against the sidewalk. It pushes so hard that the sidewalk begins to break apart!

Freezing water can change the face of the Earth.

When it rains, water gets into the small cracks in rocks. In winter, the water freezes and pushes the cracks wider apart. Then pieces of rock chip off. After thousands of years, the whole landscape may change. Some mountainsides may become more jagged. Other mountains may become worn down. Valleys may become wider.

Water can change the landscape in another way. Running water *erodes,* or wears down, certain kinds of rocks. It cuts through the rocks and makes steep river banks. Of course, this takes a very long time. It may even take millions of years. The deep, winding canyons of the American West were made this way.

What happens to all the bits of rock that are worn away?

Some are carried long distances by the running water of streams. They are mixed with mud and other materials. Then, when the streams overflow after heavy rains, part of this muddy material is left behind on the banks. It becomes rich soil and makes good farming land.

The rest of the muddy material is swept along as streams and rivers empty into the oceans. There are many minerals in this material. Some of these are salty. Did you ever go swimming in the ocean and accidentally swallow some water? If you did, you know how salty it tastes!

Why is the ocean salty?

You may wonder why the "fresh" water in rivers and lakes does not taste salty, too. Here is a simple experiment that will help you understand why ocean water is saltier than fresh water.

Pour about a tablespoon of water into a saucer. Then add a quarter of a teaspoon of salt. Mix the salt with the water until the salt seems to disappear. It has *dissolved*, or become part of the water. Taste a drop of the water. Does it taste salty? It should. This proves the salt is still there, even though you can't see it. Now set the saucer aside for a few hours, until the water has evaporated. A white crust will be left in the saucer. Although the water has evaporated, something has remained. If you taste it, you will discover that it is salt!

As rivers flow into the ocean, they bring dissolved salt with them. But there is so little salt in the river water that you cannot taste it. As the water evaporates from the ocean, the salt remains. The ocean gets saltier and saltier, as more salt is carried to the ocean. A million years from now, the seas will be even more salty than they are today.

Whether it is salty or fresh, water is one of our most important natural resources. We need water just to stay alive. We also use water in many other ways.

What are some of the ways we use water?

People have always used water for *transportation*. Rivers are like watery roads. For thousands of years, boats have carried goods and people up and down rivers, and even across the oceans. Today, huge cargo ships move from port to port along the world's waterways.

Water is also used for *recreation*. Lakes, rivers, and seashores are popular places for vacations, because people enjoy swimming, sailing, and fishing.

Water is used in *manufacturing* and *industry*. Huge amounts of water are needed for cooling industrial machines. Every canned and bottled soft drink is made mostly of water. And it takes about 150 gallons (570 liters) of water to make the paper for *each copy* of an average-length Sunday newspaper.

People also use water for *water power*. Long ago, people learned to use the force of moving water to turn wheels. These "water wheels" were used to turn huge, round stones that ground grain into flour. Today, in many areas, water power turns the wheels of huge machines called generators. Generators produce electricity. The electricity can be sent long distances and can be used for many purposes.

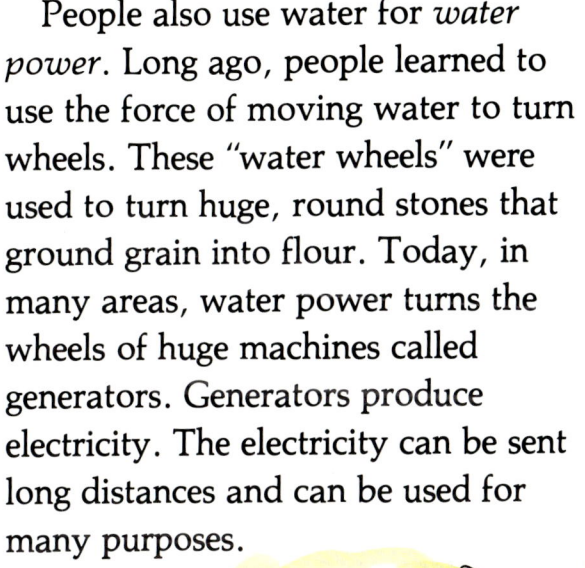

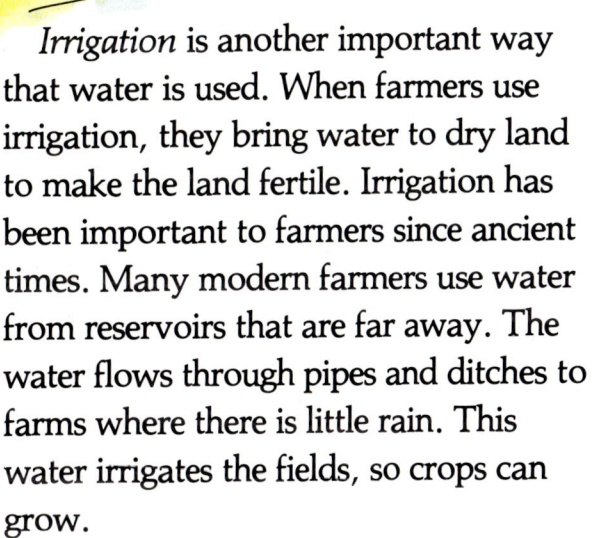

Irrigation is another important way that water is used. When farmers use irrigation, they bring water to dry land to make the land fertile. Irrigation has been important to farmers since ancient times. Many modern farmers use water from reservoirs that are far away. The water flows through pipes and ditches to farms where there is little rain. This water irrigates the fields, so crops can grow.

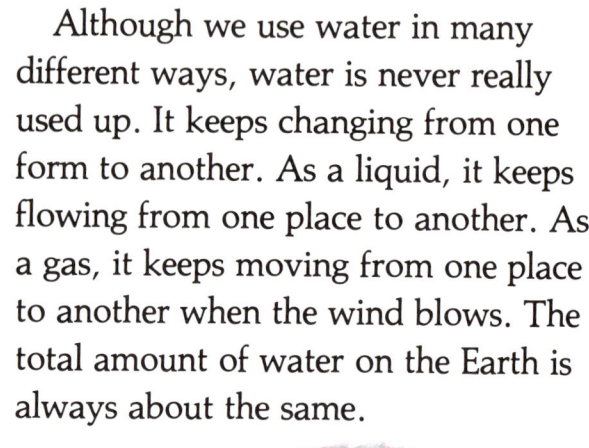

Although we use water in many different ways, water is never really used up. It keeps changing from one form to another. As a liquid, it keeps flowing from one place to another. As a gas, it keeps moving from one place to another when the wind blows. The total amount of water on the Earth is always about the same.

But in some places, there is too little water all year long. People in these places must *conserve* what they have. This means they must not waste it.

In other places, there may be enough—or too much—water in one season, but not enough during the next. In these places, the extra water from one season must be saved until later, when it is needed. One way to do this is to build a dam across a river. The water is stopped by the dam, and it forms a lake.

Special gates are built into the dam. During a dry spell, the gates are opened. Then water can flow into aqueducts and irrigation ditches. It can be used where it is needed most.

Dams can also prevent floods when there is too much rain. Because they hold back some of the extra water, dams can keep rivers from overflowing. Flood water is wasted water. It can also be very destructive. Many plants die when they receive too much water. Others are simply washed away. Many farm crops can be ruined, if fields become flooded.

Dams can prevent rivers from flooding the land. But heavy rain can cause another kind of flooding. Farmers can help prevent this kind of flooding. They can make their soil hold water, instead of letting the soil wash away in a flood of rain. One way to do this is to grow something on their fields—even if it is only grass or clover. The roots of these plants will hold the soil in place and absorb water.

    The way farmers plow their fields is also important in conserving water and preventing erosion. If farm land is on a hill, the farmer plows rows that go around the shape, or *contour*, of the hill. This is called contour plowing.

    When heavy rain falls on a hill that has been contour plowed, the water can't run straight down. Instead, it is stopped by the plants in every row. This way, the water does not wash the soil away. And the water has a better chance of sinking into the soil.

Forests help conserve water.

Have you ever gone into the woods and felt how soft, spongy, and moist the ground is under your feet? Fallen leaves, pine needles, dead plants, and the roots of living trees and plants make a carpet that holds water well.

Forests and woods do a good job of keeping water in the soil. Because they do such a good job, rainwater doesn't run straight off into rivers, where it might cause floods. Forests are important in conserving water and preventing erosion.

Conserving water is important—especially in places where there is not enough water to meet our needs. But keeping our water clean is just as important. Water that is not clean can carry germs and disease. This is called *pollution*. People everywhere are trying to prevent water pollution.

How does water become polluted?

Chemicals and other wastes from factories may pollute rivers and lakes. Many towns and cities may empty their waste water—sewage—into nearby bodies of water. Oil spills from tankers and offshore oil wells can pollute our oceans.

Saving our most precious resource

Now there are laws that prevent people from dumping chemicals and sewage into water—or even near it. Many governments are passing strict laws to keep the oceans clean. More and more people are realizing how important it is to save our most precious natural resource—water.